"Good morning Fox," said Rabbit. Fox said, "Good morning,"
then licked his lips. "You're putting on weight Rabbit, in fact
you're getting quite plump."

1

Rabbit, who didn't like Fox very much, stamped her foot and hurried down her burrow under the hedge.

Fox tried to look down the hole but it was too dark. Then he heard Rabbit singing.

"What are you doing ?" asked Badger. "Oh just listening to Rabbit singing," said Fox. "She's got a lovely voice."

"I hope you're not thinking of eating Rabbit," said Badger. "Of course not," said Fox.

"You should be more like me and eat worms and beetles," said Badger.

"I don't really like worms or beetles," said Fox. He took one more look down Rabbit's burrow then wandered off into the woods.

Rook, who had heard the animals talking, flew down into the
field. He landed on the lonely old scarecrow.

Rook watched as Rabbit came up out of her burrow and started to eat the young corn in the field. She didn't know that Fox was waiting behind a tree.

Fox crept slowly towards Rabbit. "I haven't eaten a rabbit for years," he said to himself.

Rook saw Fox coming and called out. "Fox is after you Rabbit, run away." Rabbit quickly ran behind the scarecrow.

Fox ran after her, but when he caught sight of the scarecrow he ran away.

Rook laughed so much he fell off the scarecrow with a bump. "He thought scarecrow was the farmer," shouted Rook as he flew back up. Badger saw what happened and was very cross.

13

Rabbit peeped from behind the scarecrow. "Has he gone?" she asked. "Yes, but he will be back when he is hungry," said Rook. "Oh dear," said Rabbit.

"I've got an idea," said Badger. "If Fox is frightened of the scarecrow, then Rabbit should build her burrow near to the scarecrow." So Rabbit dug a new burrow.

15

Fox didn't come near Rabbit again. She's quite safe now and the scarecrow likes the company.